IDENTIFYING RADIO PROCEDURES FOR PILOTS

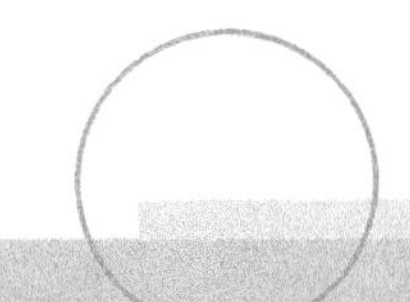

Compiled by: Talking Radio

TABLE OF CONTENT

ABBREVIATIONS

AFI	Africa Indian Ocean Region
ATIS	Automated Terminal Information Service
ATSU	Air Traffic Services Unit
IATA	International Airline Transport Association
IFR	Instrument Flight Rules
MTOW	Maximum Take Off Weight
PTT	Push to Talk
RT	Radio Telephony
VDF	VHF Directional Finder
VHF	Very High Frequency
VFR	Visual Flight Rules

1. VDF and associated RT Phraseology	**Brief Overview**
	The VHF Directional Finder, (VDF) is a ground-based radio aid type equipment, located in the vicinity of the Control Tower, that assists the ATC in identifying the position of an Aircraft when unable to utilize additional resources such as primary or secondary radar. It is activated once the PTT switch of the transceiver is selected **by the Pilot** to make a transmission.
2. Airspaces (Controlled and Uncontrolled RT)	**Brief Overview**
	The radio procedures in Controlled Airspace require two-way radio communications with ATC who supply an Air Traffic Control service, however when flying in Uncontrolled Airspace it is the Pilots responsibility to make these transmissions containing their intentions, altitude, routing, etc. A Pilot is therefore responsible for their own separation and collision avoidance without ATC support when flying in uncontrolled airspace.

3. General terms associated with (RT) Phraseology	**Brief Overview**
	RT terms need to be managed in a professional manner which includes radio check compliance, etiquette, monitoring and the associated applications in compliance with standard terminology. The radio telephony terminologies that are used by Pilots and ATC`S can be referenced in ICAO Document 4444. Student Pilots are introduced to numerous Radio Telephony terms during the course of their Pilot License training, (VFR) which they will utilize when flying circuit training for example, and they will progress with the application of RT terminologies as they progress to Instrument flying training (IFR).
4. Radio Telephony (RT) Phraseology : Non-Radar environment	**Brief Overview**
	RT is crucial in a non-radar environment, particularly so due to the fact that the ATC managing this Airspace is not able to utilize radar as a resource, or form of reference to identify the position

	of the Air traffic that they are speaking to at any stage. RT within this type of environment is generally lengthy and contains lots of pertinent information by the transmitting party/ies. The ATC's ability to detect a navigational error and resolve collision hazards is seriously degraded should a deviation from a clearance occur in a non-radar environment.
5. Radio Telephony (RT) Phraseology - Radar environment	**Brief Overview**
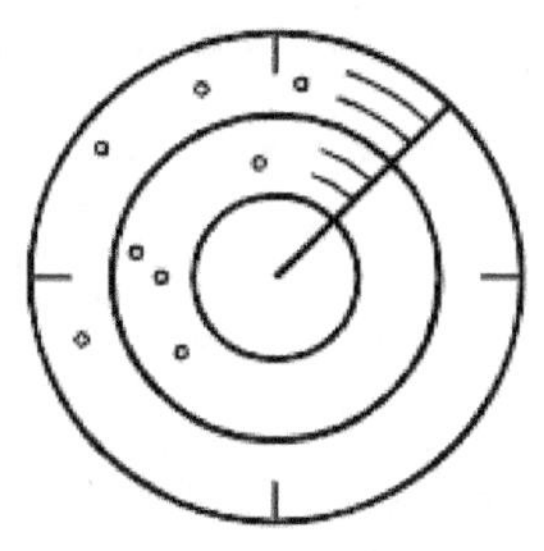	Since ATC can pro-actively manage an Airspace that is equipped to provide a radar control service, there is generally an increase in traffic movements throughout a Radar equipped environment. They are collectively climbing, descending or flying straight and Level at any given stage, and ATC manages separation between all these aircraft through set applications which includes shortened RT procedures to keep the frequency less saturated for uninterrupted transmission purposes.

6. Relaying of messages for other Stations on frequency	**Brief Overview**
	A situation could arise where an Aircraft is unable to establish contact with another party on frequency, say the Tower for example. This could be due to conditions such as high ground that are affecting the signal transmission (Line of Sight). In this instance the relay of your transmission through a party that is in contact with the Tower frequency ensures that the message is transmitted to the intended party when you are unable to.
7. Radio Telephony (RT) Phraseology - Uncontrolled Frequency Broadcasts	**Brief Overview**
	Transmissions that are made in Uncontrolled Airspace by the Pilot should contain information that indicates their intentions throughout any stage of their flight. The pilot is ultimately responsible for their safety, as well as those flying within the same Airspace limits at the time. They therefore need to ensure

		these broadcasts are made accurately, and as often as is deemed required.
8.	Radio Telephony (RT) Phraseology - IATA Inflight Broadcast Procedure (IFBP)	**Brief Overview**
		The content of an In-Flight Broadcast Procedure (IFBP), which is similar to that of a transmission made by a Pilot when flying in Uncontrolled Airspace, is made by the Pilot at least 10 minutes prior to entering, during and prior to exiting designated Africa Indian Ocean Region (AFI) Airspace. The broadcast must be clearly pronounced in English. This measure has been introduced due to communication facilities affecting certain Flight Information Regions resulting in limited ATC services.
9	Radio Telephony (RT) Phraseology - ATIS	**Brief Overview**
		The ATIS can be summarized as a group of selected information which is passed to the listener on frequency collectively represented by a designated letter from the Phonetic

	Alphabet. This information is updated by the service provider every thirty minutes and is continually made available as a voice information package on the ATIS under the next letter that follows in the phonetic alphabet. NOTE: Digital – ATIS (D-ATIS) is also supplied by those service providers at Airfields where this equipment is fitted, and available.
10. Radio Telephony (RT) Phraseology – PIREPS	**Brief Overview**
	A Pilot Report or PIREP is a report of the actual weather conditions as encountered by an aircraft whilst in flight. These reports are generally transmitted by radio to an appropriate ground station for further management thereof but, dependent on the situation at the time, they can also be made by telephone after landing. Pilots are encouraged to transmit this information to all parties on frequency as soon as it is known. This weather information needs to be as accurate as possible, so the pilot intending to make the PIREP transmission needs to

	make sure of their broadcast as this information can be of value to other parties who may potentially be affected by it.
11. Transponder related Radio Telephony (RT) Phraseology	**Brief Overview**
	A discreet transponder code, (often called a squawk code), is assigned by air traffic controllers to uniquely identify an aircraft when using Radar to provide an ATC service. In terms of RT related to Transponder Operations, the term `SQUAWK` is used in numerous transmissions which refers to the communication that comes from an aircraft's transponder, i.e. - the radio equipment that a plane is fitted with that allows it to communicate with the radar system of air traffic control on the ground. A squawk code is related to procedures when flying in a radar environment where the ATC can identify the aircraft on radar and place them for example under radar control on frequency. Any RT related to transponders contains the term `Squawk` in each such transmission.

12. TCAS related Radio Telephony (RT) Phraseology	**Brief Overview**
	A Traffic Collision Avoidance System (TCAS) Resolution Advisory (RA), is a warning to the Pilot of an immediate risk of collision. It is therefore essential that all activities connected with response to a TCAS RA should ideally make a positive contribution to collision avoidance. For this reason, RT phraseology in a transmission associated with TCAS, specifically `TCAS RA`, which identifies a pending emergency, must be clear, precise and unambiguous. Please note that the instruction received by the Pilot from the TCAS equipment in the aircraft's cockpit, always overrides any ATC instruction that is connected to this air traffic resolution period.
13. `Q` CODES and Radio Telephony (RT) Phraseology	**Brief Overview**
	The Q codes were originally developed to facilitate communication between maritime radio operators speaking different languages.

	Gradually this system was also introduced into the Aviation sector. Q codes are three-letter codes starting with the letter Q used in radio communication. Although there are now limited Q codes still utilised in radio telephony communication within the Aviation sector, those that are still in force are used in radiotelephony conversations with air traffic control as a form of \`unambiguous shorthand\`, where safety and efficiency are of vital importance.
14. Radio Telephony (RT) Phraseology - Wake Turbulence related	**Brief Overview**
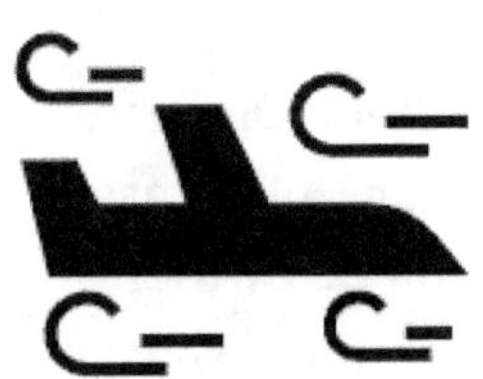	ATC makes use of this specific RT when cautioning aircraft about wake turbulence that may affect their departure path of flight. This is particularly significant for example when a light aircraft departs behind a medium or heavy aircraft category. On being cautioned by ATC about the possible affect that the wake turbulence may generate, that pilot has the option of advising ATC that they intend holding their position on the ground for an indefinite period prior to getting airborne. Note that Air

	traffic controllers play a large role in assuring that aircraft avoid wake turbulence since pilots are unable to visually identify this phenomenon. RT instructions need to be clearly transmitted by ATC when applying wake turbulence separation, and avoidance instructions.
15. Radio Telephony (RT) Phraseology - Emergency Procedures	**Brief Overview**
	In Aviation, an emergency condition is classified in accordance with the degree of danger or hazard being experienced. This can be classified as either a Distress or Urgency Situation. A Distress situation is signified by the International RT term `Mayday` spoken 3 times followed by the distress information/content dependant on the situation, while an Urgency situation is signified by the International RT term `Pan-Pan` spoken 3 times and then also followed by the urgency information/content dependant on the situation. Although the International VHF

	Aeronautical frequency 121.5 MHz is specifically for emergency broadcasts, the Pilot can make an emergency transmission on any VHF frequency dependant on the situation being experienced at that time. When an emergency is taking place on frequency, all non-essential pilots/operators need to maintain a listening watch on the emergency frequency, and not broadcast unnecessarily.
16. Radio Telephony (RT) Phraseology - Radio Communication Failure Procedures	**Brief Overview**
	It is imperative that the pilot experiencing a possible Radio Communications Failure (RCF), continues to make transmissions on all available frequencies, dependant on the emergency situation being experienced at the time. This is done in order to attempt to raise possible communication with other parties that may be listening out. Please note that during an RCF, A pilot's receiver may be faulty however their transmitter could be fully operational and thus allowing their individual

	broadcasts to be heard. Do not stop broadcasting just because you believe you have a possible radio failure. Rather consider broadcasting on all possible alternate frequencies if the situation allows
17. Radio Telephony (RT) Phraseology - RVSM Procedures	**Brief Overview**
	In order to comply with RVSM Airspace, there are certain parameters that need to be implemented by the Pilot/Operator for any pressurised aircraft that can climb to, (and beyond), the assigned RVSM Flight Levels, i.e. (F290 – F410). One of these requirements is that the Pilot needs to be familiar with specific RT procedures during RVSM, which is listed in ICAO Annex 6. These RT procedures need to be included in the companies Standard Operating Procedures, (SOP) Manual for familiarization purposes. As with Transponder RT (i.e. – Squawk), the term `RVSM` is incorporated in all Reduced Vertical Separations Minima RT.

INTRODUCTION

This RadioTelephony (RT) Procedures Study Guide has been developed from my operational experience as an ATC and RT Examiner at multiple Air Traffic Service units, backed by associated ICAO documentation as a reliable source of reference. The intention of this guide is to introduce Pilots to a host of communication requirements and procedures on frequency, related to various instruments or scenarios within the aviation context. The focus of this Guide is to highlight the importance to all Aviators regarding understanding RT, and how applying it correctly contributes significantly to maintaining a professional relationship on frequency.

The content of this booklet covers associated Radio Telephony transmissions as applied within the framework of both Controlled, and Uncontrolled Airspace.

When reviewing the content of a Radio Telephony license, it is imperative that the user of RT for Commercial Operations, (in accordance with the requirements as stipulated in ICAO Document 4444), also has knowledge of the airspaces that they are flying in, as well as the associated technical procedures, that are to be complied with when operating any aircraft.

Radio Telephony should not be labelled as merely a tool that guides you on what to say on an Aeronautical Radio, it should also be seen as a path towards understanding each environment that you could potentially find yourself operating in at any stage, so that you are well prepared to communicate on frequency whenever required.

This outlook includes, for example, when:

- Starting your Aircraft's engines,

- whilst in flight.

- preparing to approach and land,

in order to be able to apply the correct RT procedures on frequency.

The issuing of an Aeronautical RT license indicates that you are legally competent to communicate on an Aeronautical VHF radio subject to your Visual Flight Rules, (VFR) and/or Instrument Flight Rules (IFR) operator competency.

Note:

In most States across the Globe, the applicant for an Aeronautical radio license is also required to be found competent with the practical communication component of the Radio Telephony assessment, (in addition to the theory testing requirements), prior to being issued with the relevant Aeronautical RT License and/or Pilots License.

After you have been issued with a RT License, it does not normally require any form of proficiency renewal, (subject of course to a regulatory intervention for that license concerned) however, should you relocate to another State at any stage, then as part of your flying competency requirements, you may need to also ensure that you are appropriately licensed to comply with procedures for that State concerned by following their published procedures, in order to apply for the relevant radio license.

In other words, the privileges of an Aeronautical RT license that you are to be issued with, will only permit you to make use of it

in an aircraft that is registered for that State in which the radio license has originally been issued.

All the best with your professional RT communications studies and we are confident that this Study guide will help expand your knowledge within the framework of RT.

P.S. - This study guide includes sample RT transmissions, where appropriate, that illustrate the relevant description for each.

P.P.S. – Should you wish to find out more about the training services that we have to offer, or how to go about improving your RT skills, please email dylan@talkingradio.net

CHAPTER 1

The VHF Directional Finder (VDF) and associated RT Phraseology

The VHF Direction Finder (VDF) is a Navaid that uses the communication signals of an aircraft in flight to obtain their approximate azimuth (bearing). This is generally utilised to assist aircraft in flight that appear to be lost and/or in distress.

The VDF basically works as follows: When the pilot selects their Push to Talk (PTT) on the radio transceiver the VDF unit at the Air Traffic Services Unit receives the signal from the aircraft and then sends it to a VHF receiver that displays the approximate direction from where that transmitting aircraft is emitting on the electronic readout of the appropriate VDF unit as a bearing.

The readout will reflect either the aircrafts bearing from the station, or it's bearing to the station and is dependent on the selected 'Q' code as determined by the ATC working from a Controlled Aerodrome. (See table that follows)

QDM	Magnetic bearing to the Station
QDR	Magnetic radial from the station
QTE	True bearing of aircraft from a station
QUJ	True heading to steer to the Station

ATC needs to ideally first review this information received, prior to issuing any further instructions to the pilot utilising the selected 'Q' code as per the VDF, in order to facilitate them further. The current heading of the aircraft that is presumed lost, based on multiple staggered VHF transmissions to this aircraft, from ATC, will assist with the formulating of this information. This includes transmissions from the ATC to the Pilot such as:

ATC INSTRUCTION	PILOTS REPLY
`ABC report your heading'	`ABC Heading 070`
* VDF Indicates Heading 180	

ATC INSTRUCTION	PILOTS REPLY
'ABC report number of people on board'	`ABC 2 POB`
*VDF Indicates Heading 210	

ATC INSTRUCTION	PILOTS REPLY
'ABC confirm fuel endurance'	`ABC has 1-hour fuel remaining`
*VDF Indicates Heading 240	

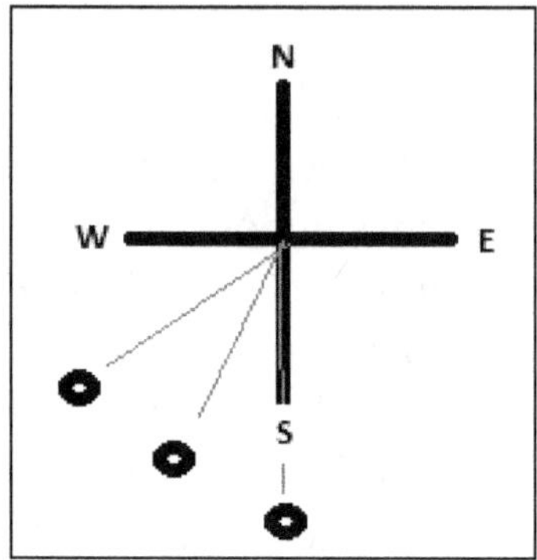

From these 3 headings, obtained through this demonstration process following the VDF heading readouts, it can then be ascertained that this aircraft, presumed to be lost, is routing in a West South West (WSW) direction. This is based on the subsequent replies from the pilot to each ATC request, resulting in a specific heading depicted on the VDF as an outcome.

CHAPTER 2

Airspaces (Controlled and Uncontrolled RT)

Controlled & Uncontrolled

Objectives of Air Traffic Control

The objectives of Air Traffic Services are to:

• Prevent collisions between Aircraft;

• Prevent collisions between Aircraft on the Maneuvering Area and between Aircraft and obstructions on the Maneuvering Area; Expedite and maintain a safe and orderly flow of Air Traffic;

• Provide advice and information useful for the safe and efficient conduct of Flights;

• Notify appropriate organization's concerning Aircraft in need of Search and Rescue (SAR), and to assist such organizations as required.

The meaning of Air Traffic Services

Air traffic service is a generic term meaning variously:

• Air traffic control service

• Flight Information Service

• Alerting Service

ICAO airspace classification and associated air traffic services

Most countries are member of the International Civil Aviation Organization (ICAO) and as such have signed the "Chicago Convention 1944 Aviation rules and regulations which are based on the recommendations of the ICAO.

ICAO Annex 11: Air Traffic Services, Chapter 2, Section 2.6 describes the classifications of airspaces classes A - G and the services the pilot may expect from air traffic control. (The relevant chart depicting various Airspace types follows).

Airspace Structure

Any airspace within a particular State is divided into flight information regions (FIR). Each of these regions comprises of both controlled and uncontrolled airspace. These airspaces are further compartmentalized into classes in which specific procedures are applied with respect to the management for that air traffic concerned:

Recognition of airspace/ classes of airspace on aeronautical charts

Aeronautical Charts provide information which allows pilots to track their position, and in turn provides crucial information in support of Air safety. The most common scale is 1:500,000 {1 inch = 6.86 Nautical miles (NM)}, which allows for very detailed information to be made available to the user. The World Aeronautical Chart on the other hand, (scale of 1: 1000 000), is designed to cover a larger area and is therefore less detailed. Please note that making use of an obsolete chart for navigation purposes is extremely dangerous so always take note of its publication date.

Mandatory radio communication in controlled airspace

When flying into airspace that is under the authority of Air Traffic Control (ATC), two-way radio communication is mandatory unless prior arrangements have been made.

When you receive an instruction from ATC, you shall comply, so long as your subsequent compliance does not violate regulations or create any unsafe condition.

Remember, if you cannot comply with instructions from ATC, advise the controller of this as soon as it is possible to do so, and await their revised instruction.

Whenever you receive a transmission from ATC, you are required to respond. The nature of your responses is essential to the efficient operation of the air traffic control system. Keep your transmissions as brief as possible, but make sure you communicate your understanding of the controller's instructions. It is best to repeat the controller's instructions in order to assure them that you understand. Also consider being brief in your communication, to avoid unnecessary congestion on the frequency.

Mandatory radio communication in advisory airspace

In advisory, (or uncontrolled) airspace, all pilots are responsible for their own separation and collision avoidance. Where so provided in this airspace, Air traffic control will provide IFR aircraft with traffic information on other IFR and VFR aircraft in the area. These aircraft are then required to use this traffic information to maintain enough separation from one other. It is very poor airmanship for a pilot to not broadcast their intentions on the relevant frequency while operating in this type of airspace. Pilots operating in this type of airspace are reminded to remain up to

date with local TIBA frequencies for that uncontrolled section of airspace concerned.

Compliance with rules of air and air traffic control clearances and instructions

Voice communications:

When an ATC clearance has been obtained, no pilot in command may deviate from that clearance unless an amended clearance is obtained, an emergency exists, or the deviation is in response to a traffic alert and collision avoidance system resolution advisory.

However, except in Class A airspace, a pilot may cancel an IFR flight plan if the operation is being conducted in VFR weather conditions. When a pilot is uncertain of an ATC clearance, that pilot shall immediately request clarification from ATC.

In order to cancel an IFR flight plan on frequency, the Pilot needs confirmation of this from ATC, as per the example below:

PILOT	ATC
`Approach, ABC has the airfield in sight, request to cancel IFR this time`	
	`ABC, IFR cancelled at time 1022, descend VFR to 2500 feet, report right downwind runway 19`
IFR cancelled at time 1022, descend VFR to 2500 feet,	

report right downwind runway 19, ABC`	

Unless otherwise authorized by ATC, no person operating an aircraft may operate that aircraft according to any clearance or instruction that has been issued to the pilot of another aircraft for air traffic control purposes.

Each pilot in command who, in an emergency, or in response to a traffic alert and collision avoidance system resolution advisory, deviates from an ATC clearance or instruction, shall notify ATC of that deviation as soon as possible.

Except in an emergency, no person may operate an aircraft contrary to an ATC instruction in an area in which air traffic control is exercised.

CHAPTER 3

General terms associated with RT

Time

UTC is the time standard commonly used across the world. The world's timing centres have agreed to keep their time scales closely synchronized - or coordinated - therefore the name Coordinated Universal Time has been agreed upon by all parties. This 24-hour time standard is kept using highly precise atomic clocks combined with the Earth's rotation. UTC is the time standard commonly used across the world for the past 50 years. It is used by meteorologists plus the aviation industry and is informally known as Zulu Time to avoid confusion about time zones and daylight-saving time.

UTC is commonly referred to as Greenwich Mean Time (GMT). UTC uses 24-hour time notation and is based on the local standard time on the zero-longitude meridian which runs through

Greenwich, England, hence, Greenwich Mean Time. Midnight in Greenwich corresponds to 00:00 UTC, noon corresponds to 12:00 UTC, and so on. It is a universal "reference" time so anyone who uses it has a "point in time" reference to a specific location.

Morse code

This a method of transmitting text information as a series consisting of on-off tones, lights, or clicks that can be directly understood by a skilled listener or observer. They make use of a Morse code table while identifying the alpha-numerical components of the transmitted message. Pilots and Air Traffic

Controllers alike need only have a cursory understanding of this code which can then be used to identify Aeronautical navigational aids, such as VORs and NDBs. Station identification letters are shown on air navigation charts which correspond with the title associated with the relevant nav. aid.

Standard speech abbreviations (words and phrases)

The following Radio Telephony terms that appear below are deemed to be some of the most common generic RT phrases for all the associated disciplines covering Lower and Upper Airspace:

RT TERM	MEANING
Copied	All understood
Affirm	Yes
Negative	No
Say Again	Repeat your previous message
Correction	An error has been made in my transmission

RT in the circuit pattern forms part of the most common Radio Telephony terminologies used in Aviation:

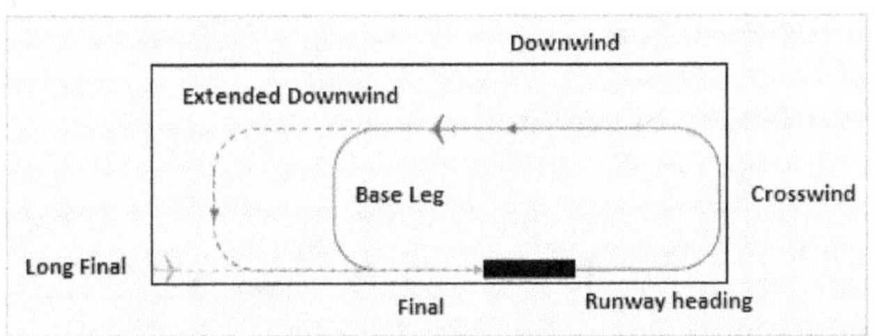

Air Traffic Services/ATU Callsigns

In terms of an Air Traffic Unit (ATU), it is important for the Pilot to address that controller by the sector that is appropriate to their designated airspace. This is referenced as follows:

ATZ/CTR	Tower
TMA	Approach
CTA	Area

NOTE: The ATZ/CTR can comprise of additional ATC positions that manage a certain part of the operation dependant on the requirements for that Airfield operation; i.e. :

TITLE	AIRSPACE MANAGEMENT
CLEARANCE DELIVERY (CLD)	This ATC issues the Pilot with their departure clearance while they are still parked in their bay/gate.
GROUND MOVEMENT CONTROL (GMC)	This ATC issues the Pilot with taxi instructions on the Maneuvering area.

Test procedures and Readability Scale

The international readability scale has been designed and implemented to facilitate both Pilots and ATC when testing the audio strength and clarity of their radio's transmission.

Broken down into 5 different levels , each section identifies all the above through a definition that has been formulated to describe it most accurately.

Strength 1 – Unreadable

This means that the receiving party is unable to hear anything on frequency as the transmission is distorted with lots of background noise.

Sometimes this is also referred to as a 'carrier wave' – i.e. no modulation.

Strength 2 – Readable now and then

This means that the receiving party can make out some of the words been spoken at times only, and the transmission clarity is hampered by a lot of static and background noise.

Strength 3 – Readable with difficulty

This means that the receiving party can make out most of the words that are transmitted on frequency, however it is still hampered by a lot of static and background noise.

(Note – As it is most common for a pilot to conduct a radio check with ATC while still on the ground, i f your transmission is determined to be between strength 1 – 3, ATC may refuse your request to start and taxi.)

Strength 4 – Readable

This means that the receiving party can understand the relevant transmission and, although it is not always clear (possibly due to the line of sight being affected), it is acceptable to maintain a two - way communication.

Strength 5 – Perfectly readable

This means that the receiving party can clearly understand the relevant transmission/s that are being made. Generally, this type of transmission is determined when an aircraft is in flight and the line of sight is less likely to be affected by possible obstacles.

To listen to an example of each of these audio transmissions please log onto the Talking Radio YouTube Channel: https://www.youtube.com/c/TalkingradioCoZa/videos

Listening out requirements and establishing of contact

It is essential for all pilots in flight to maintain a continuous listening out watch on the appropriate Aeronautical VHF frequency/ies. This means that the pilot, like the ATC, is to ensure that their volume control is not turned down to a point where they are not able to hear transmissions been made by any other parties.

When establishing initial contact with ATC the pilot must use their full callsign. In other words, they need to ensure that they include the country of registration into their initial callsign; for example: V5-ABC.

The reason for this is that everyone needs to take into account that their registered callsign is not unique and, that by not attaching the letters associated with the country where this particular aircraft has been registered, there is the possibility that another aircraft with the same callsign may be on frequency at that same space in time. The callsigns used incorrectly in this instance could result in an unsafe situation on frequency. Once you have established contact with ATC using your full callsign they will then reply to you using those parts of your callsign not

affiliated to those letters in your callsign that correspond to the country of registration.

1. Establishing Contact:

PILOT	ATC
`Tower...ZSABC`	
	`ABC...Tower`

The only time when this type of response from ATC does not occur is when two aircraft of similar callsigns are on the same operational frequency at the same time. Let's take a look at such an example:

ZS-ABC and V5-ABC make contact with ATC at the same time. ATC responds to both callsigns by coupling each as follows:

The callsign ZSABC is regrouped and transmitted as ZSC

The callsign V5ABC is regrouped and transmitted as V5C

In this instance notice that the ATC has taken the first two, and last letters of each callsign and regrouped the letters to make a callsign appropriate to that specific aircraft. In so doing they have ensured that there is no possibility of any ambiguity or confusion arising during subsequent transmissions with either of these aircraft.

If you are operating a non-schedule (charter) or schedule flight, then your aircraft registration must be replaced by the operator callsign for that particular flight. For example – TR012, pronounced – Talking Radio 012. It is important to use the full callsign that has been assigned to your flight in this instance as opposed to just using part of it; such as 012. The reason for this is that there is a possibility that another aircraft with a similar callsign is operating in this airspace and transmitting on that same operational frequency at the time, such as BA012. This could ultimately lead to lots of confusion/ambiguity on the frequency for all concerned and render the situation as potentially unsafe.

2. Acknowledgement of receipt

Pilots are encouraged to reply back to an ATC's transmission by either:

i)   Reading back their callsign in the event that ATC is only transmitting information to them.

ii)   Reading back an instruction followed by their callsign.

Note that 2 clicks on frequency is NOT an indication of acknowledgement of receipt.

Corrections and Repetitions

It is imperative that you make use of the RT term 'CORRECTION' when correcting your own transmission on frequency as failure to do so can result in confusion occurring.

3. Correcting your RT transmission

Incorrect RT transmission	Correct RT transmission
`Approach ABC heading 120, *UHMM*, 150`	
	`Approach ABC heading 120 <u>Correction</u> 150`

It must be noted that ATC will also repeat a transmission to a Pilot when they want to ensure that:

i)   It is understood if there is any possibility of uncertainty arising at any given period

ii)   The pilot has the opportunity to hear it being repeated. (In this instance the Pilot will ask ATC to 'Say Again')

iii)   It is read back correctly if this was not done on the initial readback reply transmission by the Pilot.

CHAPTER 4

RT (Non-Radar)

The use of RT in a non-radar environment is paramount in ensuring that the ATC managing this particular Airspace can facilitate a safe service to all Air traffic on their frequency. In a Non-radar environment, the ATC's ability to detect a navigational error and resolve a potential collision is seriously degraded when any deviation from their clearance occurs. It is therefore imperative that the Pilot ensures constant accuracy in all their actions and, similarly, asks the ATC on frequency for confirmation of any instruction that they may be unsure of.

In the simulated exercises that follow we will demonstrate the application of RT being applied accurately;

EXERCISE ONE:

RT (SIMULATED) FOR TRAFFIC FLYING IN A PROCEDURAL / (NON-RADAR)   CONTROLLED ENVIRONMENT

Objective – To communicate with Approach control in a combined Ground/Tower/Approach frequency environment.

NOTE:

The flight plan that has been filed for this flight has requested to route to the facilities VOR and enter the hold for one approach to the active runway followed by a full stop.

This exercise is designed around a fictitious airfield, (Talking Radio), for training purposes;

ESTABLISHING CONTACT WITH TOWER

PILOT	ATC
`Talking Radio Tower good day, ZSABC`	
	`ABC, Tower`
`ABC, in bay A7 requests start as per flight plan reference number EL01`	
	`ABC, Information Charlie, QNH 1021, start approved, report ready for taxi`
`Information Charlie, QNH 1021, start approved, will call ready for taxi, ABC`	

REPORTING READY FOR TAXI

PILOT	ATC
`Tower, ABC ready f or taxi`	
	`ABC, taxi Bravo to the CAT 1 ILS holding point runway 35, cross runway 27, report ready to copy your clearance`
Taxi Bravo to the CAT 1 ILS holding point runway 35,	

cross runway 27, will report ready to copy clearance, ABC`	

NOTE: *In this exercise the Pilot will obtain the clearance from ATC while on the taxi, however the more preferred process is to issue to pilot with their clearance while they are still in their parking bay, prior to the actual start and taxi phase.*

READY TO COPY ATC CLEARANCE

PILOT	ATC
`Tower, ABC ready to copy clearance`	
	`ABC cleared for the training flight runway 35 non-standard, after departure maintain runway heading, climb to 6500 feet, left turn intercept radial 320 climb to 8000 feet, on passing 7000 feet route direct DKV to hold`
`Cleared for the training flight runway 35 non-standard, after departure maintain runway heading, climb to 6500 feet, left turn intercept radial 320 climb to 8000 feet, on passing 7000 feet route direct DKV to hold, ABC`	

	`ABC readback correct, report ready for departure`
`Will report ready for departure, ABC`	

CONTACTING TOWER READY FOR DEPARTURE

PILOT	ATC
`Tower, ABC ready for departure`	
	`ABC, Runway 35, cleared take off, surface wind 340 degrees 12 knots, report on track DKV`
`Cleared take off, will report on track DKV, ABC`	

ON TRACK TO THE ASSIGNED FACILITY

PILOT	ATC
`Tower ABC on track DKV passing 7200 feet`	
	`ABC Report passing overhead DKV maintaining 8000 feet`

PILOT	ATC
`Will report once passing overhead DKV maintaining 8000 feet, ABC`	

OVERHEAD THE ASSIGNED FACILITY

PILOT	ATC
`ABC overhead DKV 8000 feet entering the hold`	
	`ABC enter the hold overhead DKV maintain 8000 feet, report DKV outbound ready to commence  descent`
` Enter the hold overhead DKV maintaining 8000 feet, will report ready to commence descent ABC`	

IN THE HOLD READY TO COMMENCE FURTHER DESCENT

(NOTE – In this example you are not yet ready to commence with the approach , as you are above the initial approach altitude ,or you are flying an aircraft whose performance ratio will not allow you to descend on the outbound ,and intercept for the approach on the inbound, all while having to only fly one hold).

PILOT	ATC
`ABC...DKV outbound request to descend in the hold`	
	`ABC, in the hold descend to 4500 feet, report ready to commence the approach`
`Will descend in the hold to 4500 feet and report ready to commence the Approach, ABC`	

IN THE HOLD OUTBOUND READY TO COMMENCE THE APPROACH

PILOT	ATC
`Tower, ABC is DKV outbound 4500 feet ready to commence the approach`	
	`ABC cleared for the VOR approach runway 35, report established inbound`
`Cleared for the VOR approach runway 35, report established inbound, ABC`	

ESTABLISHED INBOUND ON THE APPROACH

PILOT	ATC
`Tower ABC established inbound`	
	`ABC descend to MDA report final approach or going around`
`Descend to MDA, report final approach or going around, ABC`	

AT MDA ON FINAL APPROACH

PILOT	ATC
`Tower ABC at MDA, final approach runway 35, full stop`	
	`ABC runway 35 cleared to land surface wind calm`
`Cleared to land, ABC`	

(Once your landing roll is complete, ATC will issue you with further taxi instructions)

CHAPTER 5

RT (Radar)

Unlike the RT in a Non-Radar environment, communication procedures within a Radar environment are seen to be short and concise. This can be partly attributed to the airspace complexity which in turn is based on the availability of resources such as Secondary Radar, to assist the ATC in managing a safe, orderly and expeditious flow of Air Traffic. The RT that has been developed for use within such an Airspace ensures that the frequency is `blocked` by whoever may be transmitting at the time, for a very limited period.

RT (SIMULATED) PROCEDURES FOR TRAFFIC THAT IS DEPARTING ON A SID

Objective – To communicate with Clearance Delivery, Ground, Tower and Approach control on separate frequencies.

ESTABLISHING CONTACT WITH CLEARANCE DELIVERY TO OBTAIN A CLEARANCE

PILOT	ATC
`Clearance delivery good day, VTABC`	
	`ABC, Clearance delivery, good day pass your message`

\`ABC, in bay B3, request clearance for a flight to Barnesville as per flight plan reference number JS12\`	\`ABC, cleared Jamestown to Barnesville runway 07Left standard Vasi2A departure, Flight level 100 on request, airborne frequency  124.5, squawk 4712\`
\`ABC copies cleared Jamestown to Barnesville runway 07Left standard Vasi2A departure, Flight level 100 on request, airborne frequency 124.5, squawk 4712\`	
	\`ABC readback correct, Information Bravo, QNH 1021, CTOT 1210, contact ground for start 121.9\`
Information Bravo copied, QNH 1021, * CTOT 1210, contact ground for start 121.9, ABC	

****CTOT – Calculated Take off Time***

(This is a slot allocation time calculated to determine the time by which a flight is required to become airborne).

CONTACTING GROUND FOR START

PILOT	ATC
`Ground, VTABC request start`	
	`ABC Ground, time check 0635, start approved, report ready for taxi`
`Start approved, report ready for taxi, ABC`	

REPORTING READY FOR TAXI

PILOT	ATC
`Ground, ABC ready for taxi`	
	`ABC, taxi Bravo to the CAT2 ILS holding point runway 07 Left`
`Taxi Bravo CAT 2 ILS Holding point runway 07 Left, ABC`	

AT TRANSFER POINT BETWEEN GROUND AND TOWER ATC

PILOT	ATC
	`ABC ready for departure contact Tower, 118.1`

`Ready for departure contact Tower, 118. 1, ABC`	

NOTE: *The Pilot can also call ATC on frequency to advise that they are ready for Departure and does not necessarily have to wait for ATC to initiate this transmission.*

CONTACTING TOWER READY FOR DEPARTURE

PILOT	ATC
`Tower, VTABC ready for departure`	
	`ABC, line up runway 07 Left`
`Line up runway 07 Left, ABC`	
	`ABC, runway 07Left, surface wind 030 degrees 12 knots, cleared take off`
`Cleared take off, ABC`	

CONTACTING APPROACH ON PASSING ASSIGNED ALTITUDE

For further information on RT communication associated with the Terminal Control Area, why not consider taking a look at the RT related practical communications study guides available through http://www.talkingradio.net

CHAPTER 6

Relaying of messages for other stations

There is a possibility that you may be required to relay a transmission in flight, for another party, while on a specific frequency. The reason for this could be due to any of the following factors:

i) The aircraft is out of VHF communication range

ii) The aircraft is flying at a low altitude

iii) There are numerous obstacles affecting the 'line of sight' transmission

In either instance it is good airmanship for all parties to assist, when able, with the relaying of a VHF message on frequency. ATC will also make more use of this option, asking all pilots on frequency in a particular area to assist them with the relay of a message to a specific aircraft.

Types of relay transmissions:

- **Relay request to any traffic on frequency**

PILOT	ATC
a) `All traffic on frequency, Citation ABC request relay to ATC...`	

- **Relay request to an aircraft on frequency**

PILOT	3LDEF
` 3LDEF... this is Allstar1... please relay to ATC that we request to cancel SAR at time 0920'	
	Allstar 1....3LDEF copied, your request to cancel SAR with ATC at time 0920... standby

In this example 3LDEF would proceed to make contact with the ATC Station and relay the message:

NOTE – This type of relay can only take place if:

i) The aircraft facilitating the relay has VHF contact with the requested station (In this simulated example it would be ATC).

ii) The aircraft facilitating the relay reports back to the aircraft requesting the relay, with the actual time that ATC cancelled Search and Rescue (SAR), on frequency.

CHAPTER 7

Uncontrolled frequency Broadcasts

The purpose of broadcasting on an uncontrolled frequency is to inform all parties, (known and unknown), of their intentions. This type of approach to communication assists ins maintaining safe skies, especially in an Uncontrolled airspace that does not receive a positive control service from ATC. When making such a transmission, the following information needs to be included in such a broadcast:

Their callsign?
Aircraft type? which can also be substituted with: ● 'High-Wing', 'Low-Wing' or 'Helicopter' OR ● Aircraft colour?
What is their current height?
Where are they at present?
What are their intentions?
When do they expect to broadcast next?

The uncontrolled broadcast should also ideally include the frequency that the pilot is making this transmission on, which would be included at the beginning of the broadcast itself. For example – 'Traffic on 1 … 2 … 5 … decimal …8…. '

Uncontrolled frequencies belong to a collective referred to as `Traffic Information Broadcast By All Aircraft` (TIBA). A TIBA frequency is therefore deemed as uncontrolled and would therefore be listed as such in the AIP for the State that you are operating in.

An extract from ICAO Annex 11 states that the purpose of a TIBA broadcast is to permit reports and relevant supplementary information of an advisory nature, by a pilot, on an Aeronautical VHF frequency.

Uncontrolled sectors include: (but are not limited to)

- General Flying Areas

- Traffic flying below 1500 feet AGL outside of Controlled Airspace

For all traffic flying in a designated civilian General Fly ing Area you can verify information such as the TIBA frequency to be selected, by referring to the relevant AIP.

NOTE: Any reference to a Special Flight Rules Area, (i.e. - an Airspace in which the normal regulations of flight do not apply in whole or in part), incorporates frequencies associated with TIBA.

CHAPTER 8

IATA Inflight Broadcast Procedure (IFBP) in the AFI region

A listening watch shall be maintained on a designated AFI frequency (126.9 MHz) for at least 10 minutes prior to entering the designated airspace, until such time as you have left this airspace.

- All broadcasts are to be made in English.

These broadcasts must be made at least 10 minutes prior to entering or crossing a FIR within an IFBP region. In addition, these broadcasts will also be made at the following times:

- 10 minutes prior to crossing or joining an ATS route.

- At no less than 20-minute intervals apart.

- Before any change in Flight Level.

- At any other times deemed necessary by the Pilot.

- This broadcast shall contain the following information:

- All Stations

- This is (flight number) in the (FIR name)

- Flight Level (height)

- Cardinal (Direction) on (Airway)

- Forward estimate/s (time based in UTC)

CHAPTER 9

ATIS plus associated Radio Telephony (RT) Phraseology

The Automated Terminal Information Service (ATIS) is a continuous voice broadcast, containing weather information, specific to that particular Air Traffic Services Unit (ATSU), where it is being transmitted from a dedicated frequency. The recording is updated in fixed intervals, or when there is any significant change in the relevant information, such as a change in the active runway. Nowadays some airfields also make use of Digital ATIS, (D-ATIS), which is a form of digital transmission that is basically the same supply of the updated weather information, but in a digital format.

A simulated example of the type of ATIS related weather information you can typically expect to receive from ATC on frequency is as follows:

Message	Explanation
This is <u>Talking Radio</u> International…. Information Yankee	Indicates the broadcast is for aircraft inbound to Talking Radio Airport and the Bulletin's identification letter
Main landing runway 29	Main <u>runway</u> used for landing is 29, which indicates the direction (290 degrees magnetic)
Transition level 90	When descending below Flight Level 90 (equivalent to 9000ft altitude on a

	standard barometric setting of 1013 hPa), an aircraft should set their altimeter to the prevailing barometric pressure (QNH) of the airfield (Which is also given later in the ATIS)
Two Six Zero Degrees, One Fife knots	Wind direction from azimuth 260 degrees magnetic (West-southwest), averaging 15 knots
Visibility one zero kilometres	The visibility is Good (10 kilometers or more)
CAVOK	Ceiling and Visibility Okay (Clear Skies prevailing)
Temperature One Nine, dewpoint One Zero	Temperature and dewpoint measured in degrees Celsius
QNH One Zero Two Tree hectopascal	QNH (barometric pressure adjusted to mean sea level)
No significant change	No significant change in weather expected
End of information Yankee	End of the bulletin transmitted via either Voice ATIS OR Digital ATIS

	and the bulletin's identification letter again

ATC will pass the ATIS as a Phonetic Alphabet Collective, i.e. Alpha – Zulu, when passing the current ATS to a Pilot on frequency.

PILOT	ATC
	`DEK, Information **Yankee**… QNH1023… Contact Ground for Start… 121.9`
`Information **Yankee**… QNH1023… Contact Ground for Start… 121.9…DEK`	

CHAPTER 10

PIREPS Inflight Broadcast , Radio Telephony (RT) Phraseology

A Pilots Report (PIREP) is a report by the pilot of actual weather conditions encountered by an aircraft whilst in flight. These types of reports are normally transmitted by the Pilot to the ATC on frequency, and typically contain the following information:

- The location of the flight relative to a NAVAID or Airport

- Your current altitude

- One or more weather observations

- The time of the weather observation in UTC

In order to make such a weather report the pilot will contact the ATC on frequency and advise them that they wish to make a PIREP. An example of such a transmission is as follows:

PILOT	ATC
Talking Radio Information, Cessna GRABC, receiving Omega VOR, 121.55, with a Pilot report...	
	GRABC...Talking Radio

	Information...standingby your PIREP
Talking Radio Information... ABC... PIREP follows... ABC is approximately 3nm to the east of Omega airfield maintaining 4500 feet... at time 1245 storm observed approaching at increased speed from the east... cloud ceiling overcast at 5000 feet...	

The ATC receiving this PIREP from the Pilot will acknowledge this transmission by reading it back to the Pilot that originally passed it to them. Following that they will write this information in their Daily Occurrence Logbook and proceed to pass this weather observation to relevant Pilots flying in the area where the weather is influencing the environment.

CHAPTER 11

Transponder related Radio Telephony (RT) phraseology

A transponder is a device found in the cockpit of an aircraft that emits an identifying signal in response to an interrogating received signal. For a pilot to fly in a controlled area that has radar coverage, their aircraft needs to be equipped with a minimum of a Mode 'C' Transponder. This transponder type indicates the aircrafts altitude in addition to its present position. Transponder codes are four-digit numbers transmitted by the transponder in an aircraft, in response to a secondary surveillance radar interrogation signal, and the output displayed on the radar screen assists air traffic controllers with traffic separation. A discre et transponder code, (often called a squawk code), is assigned by air traffic controllers to uniquely identify an aircraft on Radar. This also facilitates an easier identification of aircraft on radar when utilised.

Herewith follows several RT terms related to a Transponder:

Squawk Ident	Select the `IDENT` feature displayed on the face of the Transponder
Recycle Squawk	Switch the Transponder to `Standby`, reset the four-digit Squawk Code as allocated and then Switch the Transponder back to `ALT`

Squawk Standby	Select the Transponder to `SBY`
Squawk Mode C	Select the Transponder from `ON` (which represents coding in Mode `A`), to `ALT` (which represents coding in 'Mode C`)

CHAPTER 12

TCAS/ RT phraseology

A Traffic Collision Avoidance System (TCAS) Resolution Advisory (RA) is a warning to the Pilot of an immediate risk of collision. It is therefore essential that all activities connected with response to a TCAS RA should ideally make a positive contribution to collision avoidance. For this reason, RT phraseology associated with TCAS RAs must be clear, precise and unambiguous.

It is important to note that in the event of a (RA) notification via the TCAS, the Pilot must comply with the instruction received from their TCAS, and not that of the ATC. This action will be complied with until such time as there is no longer any risk of a collision between the affected Aircraft, and the minimum separation criteria, (or greater), has been established between the original conflicting Aircraft.

Circumstance	Pilot	ATC
After a flight receives an Instruction to comply with a TCAS RA from the TCAS equipment in the cockpit	TCAS RA	Roger OR Copied
After the response to a TCAS RA is completed, and a return to the ATC	Clear of conflict returning to (assigned clearance)	Roger OR Copied (and/or

Clearance or Instruction is initiated		Alternative Instruction)
After the response to a TCAS RA is completed and the assigned ATC clearance or instruction has been resumed	CLEAR OF CONFLICT *(assigned clearance)* RESUMED	Roger OR Copied *(and/or alternative instruction)*
After an ATC clearance OR Instruction which is contradictory to the TCAS RA received, the Flight crew will follow the RA and inform ATC directly on frequency	UNABLE…TCAS RA	Roger OR Copied

CHAPTER 13

Q Codes

The Q codes were originally developed to facilitate communication between maritime radio operators speaking different languages. Gradually this system was also introduced into the Aviation sector.

Although there are now limited Q codes still utilised in aviation radio telephony communication, those that are still in force, are used in radiotelephony conversations with air traffic control as a form of `unambiguous shorthand`, where safety and efficiency are of vital importance.

These Q Codes refer to pressure settings and are listed as follows:

QNH – Atmospheric Pressure Setting referenced as a Height above Mean Sea Level.

QFE – Atmospheric Pressure Setting referenced as a Height above Ground Level.

QNE – The Standard Atmospheric Pressure Setting of 1013.25 hPa.

NOTE: Additional reference is made in Chapter 1 of this Study Manual with regards to 4 `Q Codes` already mentioned, that are still in use.

In Controlled Airspace ATC will always supply the QNH as part of their joining or departure clearance. This is in contrast with QFE

and QNE which will only be passed to the pilot by ATC on frequency upon request.

PILOT	ATC
	`DEK, join and report left downwind runway 12, QNH 1018`
`Join left downwind runway 12, QNH 1018... DEK`	

NOTE: The QNH will also be supplied to all pilots on frequency in Controlled Airspace, by ATC, whenever the pressure setting changes by 1 hPa or greater.

PILOT	ATC
	`All traffic on 118.1...Talking Radio Tower   check QNH now 1019`
`DEK copied QNH 1019`	

CHAPTER 14

Wake Turbulence Radio Telephony (RT) Phraseology

Wake turbulence is turbulence that forms behind an aircraft as it passes through the air. ICAO mandates separation minima based upon wake turbulence categories (WTC) that are, in turn, based upon the Maximum Take Off Weight/Mass (MTOW) of the aircraft.

These minima are typically categorised as follows:

Light (L)	MTOW of 7,000 kilograms or less
Medium (M)	MTOW of greater than 7,000 kilograms, but less than 136,000 kilograms;
Heavy (H)	MTOW of 136,000 kilograms or greater.

RT Associated with Wake Turbulence

ATC makes use of this specific RT when cautioning aircraft about wake turbulence that may affect their departure path of flight. This is particularly significant for example when a light aircraft departs behind a medium or heavy aircraft category. On being cautioned by ATC about the possible affect that the wake turbulence may generate, that pilot has the option of advising ATC that they intend holding their position on the ground for an

indefinite period prior to getting airborne. (In order to assess the situation with respect to the resultant effects of the wake itself.

An example of ATC cautioning the Pilot about possible wake turbulence follows:

PILOT	ATC
	ABC, Runway 06, surface wind 090 degrees 12 knots, cleared for take-off, caution wake turbulence, the preceding departing heavy rotated abeam intersection Charlie…
`Cleared take off, copied the wake, ABC`	

The Pilot may however decide to hold their position for a minute or two to allow any pending Wake Turbulence to dissipate prior to taking power and getting Airborne. The reply from the Pilot to the take clearance, (as in the example above), would be as follows:

PILOT	ATC
	ABC, Runway 06, surface wind 090 degrees 12 knots, cleared for take-off, caution wake turbulence, the preceding departing heavy rotated abeam intersection Charlie…

| Copied Tower, ABC would prefer to hold our position for another minute before getting airborne due to the possible wake. | |

In this instance ATC would cancel the departure clearance and advise the Pilot to report ready for departure.

CHAPTER 15

Radio Telephony (RT) Phraseology - Emergency Procedures

In Aviation, an emergency condition is classified in accordance with the degree of danger or hazard being experienced, and can be classified as follows:

***Distress*:**

A condition of being threatened by grave and/or imminent danger and requiring immediate assistance

***Urgency*:**

A condition concerning the safety of an aircraft or other vehicle, or of someone on board or within sight, but which does not require immediate assistance.

WHEN THE PILOT EXPERIENCES A DISTRESS SITUATION:

In radiotelephony, the spoken word f or distress is "MAYDAY", and it should be used at the commencement of the first distress communication.

The distress signal indicates that a person or station sending the signal is threatened by grave and imminent danger and requires immediate assistance

PILOT	ATC
`Mayday , Mayday , Mayday , ABC engine failure, abeam of Saint Romeo, descending through 6000 Feet, positioning to land on highway, require immediate assistance.`	
	ABC emergency copied, standingby

In this instance ATC is informing the pilot i n distress that they have copied that the pilot is in distress, and that they are standingby to assist. Whilst off frequency ATC will comply with internal standard operating procedures for emergency situations, while simultaneously maintaining a listening watch on the frequency that ABC has declared their emergency on and assist as necessary while making the emergency air traffic a priority .

WHEN THE PILOT EXPERIENCES AN URGENCY SITUATION:

PILOT	ATC
`Pan – Pan, Pan – Pan, Pan – Pan, ABC has a passenger onboard with a heart attack, diverting this time to Saint Romeo, Maintaining Flight Level 090, ETA 1204`	

	ABC emergency copied, standingby

The process followed by the ATC will be very similar to the steps mentioned earlier with reference to a Distress situation, however because the Pilot, in most instances, still has control of the Aircraft, ATC can also proceed to ask the following when the situation allows:

PILOT	ATC
	`ABC confirm Age and Gender of the Patient`

This information, once known, can then be passed on to the emergency teams on standby so that they can be better prepared for the patient on arrival.

NOTE: These emergency terms and procedures are also incorporated within the Marine Industry.

CHAPTER 16

Radio Communication Failure (RCF) RT Procedures

With regards to radio communication failure (RCF) procedures, it is imperative that the pilot experiencing the possible RCF continues to make transmissions on all available frequencies, dependant on the emergency situation being experienced at the time, in order to attempt to raise possible communication with other parties that may be listening out. Please note that during an RCF, a pilot's receiver may be faulty however their transmitter could be fully operational and thus allowing their individual broadcasts to be heard.

NOTE: If you suspect that you have an RCF always attempt to make a transmission on frequency using the following RT procedure as an example to assist you with this:

PILOT	ATC
Traffic on 122.9, this is ZMABC, broadcasting blind, suspected radio communication failure, overhead Leroy at 5000 feet, routing Samville, any traffic please advise if you read this transmission.	

If you still on the taxi at an Airfield, or at the holding point ready for departure, and experience a possible RCF, remember that you may not depart and need to return back to the parking bay the safest possible route while broadcasting your intentions blind on the operational frequency.

Remember that there are published RCF procedures for both VFR and IFR Pilots, however there are instances when a Pilot could experience a possible radio communication failure outside of these published procedures. In either instance, it is the Pilots responsibility to continue broadcasting blind on the current frequency, as well as any other possible frequencies subject to the situation being experienced at the time. There is no set time period as to how often the Pilot should make these blind broadcasts, however what is significant is that each such transmission should contain all their relevant information including:

- Who is making this transmission?

- Where is the aircraft that is making this transmission`s current position and Altitude/Flight Level?

- Why is this Aircraft making a blind transmission?

- What are the intentions of this Aircraft that is making a blind transmission?

NOTE: for more detailed information, (or as a refresher) on radio telephony associated with VFR flying in controlled and uncontrolled airspace, please take a look at our Talking Radio website to see what products the online training shop has to offer. (www.talkingradio.net)

CHAPTER 17

RVSM Radio Telephony (RT) phraseology

As a recap in brief, the Semi-Circular rule is applied in Aviation, to establish a fixed vertical separation between aircraft routing in opposite directions. The height, (or flight level to be more correct), that is chosen, is based on the intended magnetic heading of the Aircraft for any particular flight plan route.

Before the introduction of Reduced Vertical Separation Minima (RVSM), the minimum vertical height between aircraft above Flight Level 290 used to be set at 2000 Feet. With the implementation of RVSM and its associated procedures, this minimum height separation above Flight Level 290 was reduced to 1000 Feet (i.e. equal to the minimum vertical height between aircraft operating below Flight Level 290).

The rule being that RVSM would only be applied to all aircraft operating above Flight Levels 290 up to and including Flight Level 410. Once an Aircraft exceeds Flight Level 410 on the climb, the separation minima is increased to 2000 Feet between aircraft routing in opposite directions.

In order to comply with RVSM Airspace, there are certain parameters that need to be implemented by the Pilot/Operator for any pressurised aircraft that can climb to, (and beyond), those assigned RVSM Flight Levels. The table that follows highlights the various types of RT that ATC may use as part of their instruction to a Pilot when approaching, and operating within RVSM Airspace:

PILOT IS RVSM APPROVED

ATC	PILOT
`ABC Confirm RVSM Approved	*`Affirm RVSM`*

PILOT IS NOT RVSM APPROVED

ATC	PILOT
`ABC Confirm RVSM Approved	*`Negative RVSM`*

ATC Refuses to issue Clearance for a Flight into RVSM Controlled Airspace

ATC	PILOT
ABC unable clearance into RVSM Airspace, Maintain (or Descend to, or Climb to) Flight Level	*`Maintain (or Descend to, or Climb to) Flight Level …. ABC`*

Pilot reporting severe turbulence / weather affecting ability to maintain RVSM   height keeping requirements

PILOT	ATC
`ABC unable RVSM due Turbulence`	`ABC descend to Flight Level…`9which takes the flight outside of RVSM Authorised Airspace`

Pilot reporting equipment degradation below RVSM requirements

PILOT	ATC
`ABC unable RVSM due Equipment`	`ABC descend to Flight Level…`(which takes the flight outside of RVSM Authorised Airspace)`

ATC requesting the pilot to report when able to resume RVSM

PILOT	ATC
`ABC unable RVSM due Turbulence`	`ABC descend to Flight Level…`(which takes the flight outside of RVSM Authorised Airspace)

Pilot ready to resume RVSM after equipment/weather contingency

ATC	PILOT
`ABC report able to resume RVSM	`ABC ready to resume RVSM`

CONCLUSION

Radio Telephony forms an integral part w ithin the framework of Safety in Aviation, particularly from an operational perspective. Ambiguity, miscommunication and a general lack of RT understanding, creates an unsafe environment, which needs to be avoided at all costs if every Aviator makes a concerted effort and applies the correct Aeronautical RT procedures.

Although we have only used isolated RT examples for each section included in this e Book, it is important to note that in addition to the standard RT transmissions such as Affirm, Copied, etc., there are certain RT transmissions that contribute to specific situations. All pilots must therefore be careful of becoming complacent with their RT communication procedures and instead:

a) Familiarise themselves with each update that is published concerning RT procedures. This includes:

- Aeronautical Information Publication (AIP)

- Notice to Al Airmen (NOTAM)

- Aeronautical Information Circular (AIC}

- and associated Legislative documentation.

b) Listen out where possible, to an operational frequency whilst at home during your leisure time, for example.

c) Ask a qualified Flight Instructor or ATC about any RT term or transmission that you you need an explanation of for familiarization purposes.

We hope that you have enjoyed identifying with these various RT procedures plus operational processes and have a better understanding of the application thereof. Should you wish to enquire about anything related to Radio Telephony, or are looking for assistance to help improve your own personal radio skills, please feel free to email me at the following address: dylan@talkingradio.net